The Wisdom of Wing Tsun

Table of Contents

Foreword

Your work is going to fill a large part of your life, and the only way to be truly satisfied is to do what you believe is a great work. And the only way to do great work is to love what you do. If you haven't found it yet, keep looking. Don't Settle.) My friend, Carson, whom I knew when he was a very young man, finally found his work with which he loves it more than any others. Sifu Lau Congratulations!

Raymond Law

*** Raymond Law, is the ex-boss of the author when he worked in Hong Kong. Not only did he teach things one needs to know at work, he also taught many life lessons and philosophies needed in many areas of life. He is definitely the author's inspirational teacher in life.

It was a great honor for me when one of my dear mentors, Sifu Carson Lau, asked me to write this foreword to his first book. As a young Wing Tsun enthusiast, I would often see Sifu Lau in Hong Kong Wing Tsun videos and books and wonder what it would be like to train with him. Around 2002, I was elated to find out that Sifu Lau would be moving to North America right around the time that I began teaching in New York City. Little did I know that he would eventually become one of the biggest influences in my career, not just as a practitioner of the art, but more importantly, as a teacher. But at that time if you told me that one day I would write the foreword to his first book, I'd tell you that you were absolutely crazy!

I first met Sifu Lau in Texas, during the Hong Kong SARS outbreak in 2003. He was substituting for the yearly Instructor Tutorials as Grandmaster Leung Ting was unable to leave Hong Kong at that time. When I first saw Sifu Lau in action, I was incredibility impressed. Here was this dynamic practitioner of Wing Tsun tossing larger American instructors around with absolute ease. When it was my turn to Chi Sau with him, the result was the same. I could do nothing! I could feel something was different in his skills and I knew that he was the one I wanted to learn from. From that point on, I would invite him to teach in my school as well as follow him all over North America to train with him.

In the Chinese tradition, Sifu Lau can be considered a Wing Tsun uncle to me, although at times he has always been much more like a surrogate Sifu. He is more than just someone who taught me Wing Tsun programs and sparring, he has been an example to me of what it means to be a Sifu in the art. When I was new to teaching, I made a lot of mistakes. Sifu Lau gave me the perfect advice that I needed to hear in those moments. I even made some mistakes with regards to Chinese customs and culture but he corrected me firmly, but with care.

I can never repay him for those lessons as they have served me well meeting senior masters of the Hong Kong martial arts community.

The Chinese have many sayings and one of my personal favorites is gaau hok seung jeung (教學相長). This saying highlights how teaching and learning are two sides of the same coin. Teachers learn just as much from their students as well. Sifu Lau jokingly says that I have taught him American slang and culture in a way where I am “his teacher” for those things. But I don’t think teaching him funny American slang is in any way comparable to all of the lessons he has taught me. For one, Sifu Lau was the first instructor to teach me how to teach students Chi Sau sparring. He showed me how to be a good coach and develop the student’s fighting abilities so that the students also become training partners for me. In that way, he has given me the ability to learn from my own students. That ability is worth its weight in gold because it means that I can always learn something new, even if I don’t have a senior in front of me. This is a powerful life skill that can be applied outside of the world of martial arts.

As someone who has traveled to Hong Kong regularly and learned from some of the greatest Wing Tsun masters around, I can say that Sifu Lau is hands down one of the best. Rarely can you find the combination of skill, knowledge, and the ability to give it to others. Some Sifu are skillful, but don’t teach well. Some are not very skillful, but know how to explain things. Some can explain things, but can no longer demonstrate it. Sifu Lau can explain and demonstrate everything he teaches making him an elite among the elites. Treasure this book and its teachings because a teacher like Sifu Lau is extremely rare to find.

Wishing you all the best on your journey!

Sifu Alex Richter
City Wing Tsun Athletic Association, NYC

*** Alex Richter founded the New York - based City Wing Tsun Athletic Association in 2002. The majority of his early training was at Langenzell Castle, the former headquarters for the European Wing Tsun Organization. He continued his training under some of the best Hong Kong-trained instructors, including Sifu Carson Lau. Alex Richter has authored several books on Wing Tsun and also hosts the popular Kung Fu Genius Podcast on Youtube.

For almost 40 years I have had the privilege to learn from some of the best martial arts instructors. From each of them I learned so many lessons in fighting tactics, strategy and life philosophy as I advanced through my life's journey – professional and personal. During my tenure under their guidance I earned several black belts; a milestone in a journey of that particular style. But it is only in Wing Tsun and through the teachings of Sifu Carson Lau that my skills and understanding have advanced far beyond that distinguished milestone. From his example and teachings, I have become a better person, martial artist, instructor, and a more thoughtful family man.

When I first met Sifu Lau, decades ago, I knew that I was in the presence of someone special. I have seen (and felt) the incredible power and deftness with which Sifu disposes of an attack. As his student, Todai, I have seen how he coaches students through Wing Tsun difficulties by guiding them on how to correctly apply Wing Tsun principles, rather than making numerous incremental corrections. In doing so he teaches them "how to fish" being more efficient with their own effort: incredibly aligned with Wing Tsun principles of directness and simplicity.

Although his martial prowess is beyond reproach, I have found the humility and generosity of Sifu's character to be his most admirable trait. After years of Wing Tsun training, I was given the privilege to take some private instruction from Sifu, in Toronto. As is typical, the training ran late into the night and when the lesson was over I was ready to thank Sifu and head back to my hotel. Sifu, however, insisted that we must share some time together outside of the gym and invited me to midnight snack (宵夜). I see now, that Sifu was teaching me one of the many beautiful aspects of Chinese culture; benevolence. Through Wing Tsun, Sifu has brought the wisdom of Chinese culture from Hong Kong to his North American students.

In this book, Sifu shares the essence of Wing Tsun; the core principles that make Wing Tsun Kung Fu fierce and effective. In these pages are the foundations upon which core ideas can then be applied into a plethora of "techniques". Master the principles, and the possibilities are endless! It is a generous gift, as it provides the reader the essentials to evolve their abilities as their understanding grows as they train.

I hope that this book inspires and enables you on your martial arts journey, as it has for me.

Sifu Chris Mah

*** Chris Mah, is the Head Instructor of the Northfield, Illinois branch of the CWTA. He has been learning and teaching Wing Tsun Kung Fu since the early 1990's. His own martial arts journey includes a black belt in NCAA Tae Kwon Do and traditional uchi-deshi style aikido. He believes that the greatest reward in life is to overcome one's own challenges and aid others in overcoming theirs.

I've had the great fortune of training with and learning from many incredible people throughout my more than 30 years as a martial artist. Sifu Carson Lau exemplifies the best traits of a martial arts teacher. I first met Sifu Lau in the late 1990's when he was still living in Hong Kong. He came to a seminar in San Francisco and demonstrated the incredible fighting skills of Wing Tsun Kung Fu. At the time, I had already been practicing Wing Tsun for a few years. As any martial artist can tell you, every individual has a different expression, even if the art is the same. The first time I saw Sifu Lau sparring, I saw the true beauty and power of Wing Tsun.

As the years progressed, I came to a point in my martial arts journey where I decided to follow Sifu Lau and asked to be his todai - his student, and therefore, for him to be my Sifu - my teacher. Since then, nearly 10 years ago, I've had no regrets. Sifu is not only an amazingly skilled teacher, he is also an amazing fighter. That is also a rare breed. Many great fighters have struggled to teach their arts and their expressions of their art successfully. Sifu's mastery of Wing Tsun allows him to explain and demonstrate the art in a way that anyone can understand and learn from.

As impressive as his martial skills are, the only thing even more impressive is his humility and character. Sifu is a true gentleman. He's caring and friendly to everyone he meets. Whenever I visit him in Toronto and he takes us out to dinner, everywhere we go, people smile and shake his hand. He's a celebrity, not because he's a martial arts master, but because he is a respected member of his community.

I have had the honor of learning from him, not only how to be a better martial artist, but how to be a better human being. He leads by example in all that he does. I hope you find the words in this book, the lessons he has to teach, as valuable as I have.

Sifu Steve Chan

*** Steve Chan, is the head instructor of the Evanston, Illinois branch of the CWTA. He has been practicing Wing Tsun Kung Fu since 1995. His martial arts experiences includes hand to hand combat training in the U.S. Marine Corps as well as a variety of martial arts such as judo, jujitsu, escrima, tai chi, western boxing and fencing. He strongly believes in the long term benefits of martial arts training for health, safety and mental well-being.

Carson Lau

About The Author

Carson Lau, founder of Carson Wing Tsun Academy was born in Hong Kong and came to Canada, and settled in Toronto in 2002; Since then he has been teaching Wing Tsun Kung Fu, popularizing Chinese martial arts culture.

In his childhood, he idolized Bruce Lee through his movies, his books, and his magazines. He spent many long hours doing summersaults, flying kicks, and playing with a variety of martial arts weapons, imitating the great kung fu movie stars. One day, he saw Great Grandmaster Leung Ting on television demonstrating the iconic Wing Tsun Chi Sau techniques (Sticky hand sensitivity techniques) and was entranced. The very next day, he immediately went to GGM Leung Ting's Kung Fu School and became one of the students. By chance, Carson became Cheng Chuen Fun's student, (Sifu Cheng Chuen Fun is Great Grandmaster Leung Ting's younger kung fu brother or "Sidai" 師弟 in Chinese), learning Wing Tsun Kung Fu. After years of training and with the approval of his Sifu and training colleagues, Carson soon began leading his own class at the Wing Tsun Hong Kong Headquarters. This became the start of his career teaching the Wing Tsun Kung Fu System. In the beginning, Carson was only teaching part-time, but after he completed his training, he became one of the main instructors at the school. Carson also assisted in many of Great Grandmaster Leung Ting's advanced training classes for the talented and followed the Great Grandmaster all over the world to assist in seminars and demonstrations. For more than 35 years, Carson has been teaching Wing Tsun Kung Fu with unwavering dedication, gaining the admiration of peers and other instructors alike.

Introduction

I have read many books. This is my first attempt at writing one to share with you all on a subject I care deeply about. It is very difficult to know where to begin, regardless of the subject. Please forgive me in advance for any inadequacy you may come across.

When friends caught wind of my intentions of writing a book, they inquired whether it would be a biography of my life. Like many others, I have experienced a lot in my life. I have gone through many turmoils and made forever life-altering decisions, both in my personal life and professional life as a martial art instructor. I have triumphed through many obstacles and experienced many hardships. In regards to my personal life, my martial arts career, and as a human being, I feel that there are still many more life lessons to learn, and long roads to travel. For these reasons, I do not think that this is an appropriate time to write a biography just yet, maybe in due time.

From the moment I became a Wing Tsun Kung Fu instructor to the time when I opened my own martial art gym, I always wanted to write a book on traditional idioms, quotes, and sayings that are in direct relation to the Wing Tsun Kung Fu System, the martial art that I dedicated my whole life to. The idioms of the Wing Tsun Kung Fu System are what I want to share. These idioms will not only provide practitioners with a clearer understanding of applications and techniques in the Wing Tsun Kung Fu System but they can also be applied to one's everyday life. I hope the words in these pages may inspire one's way of life for the better as they have inspired me on how I live mine.

From Ip Man opening his first Wing Chun school in Hong Kong in the 1950s to being recognized as the man who taught Bruce Lee; it didn't take long for the Wing Chun Kung Fu style to become famous around the world. With a fast, direct, and simple approach, one can see why Wing Chun Kung Fu ranks as one of the most practical and realistic forms of self-defense systems in the world. In addition, with the help of movies and decorated actors portraying Ip Man on screen, the Wing Chun Kung Fu style reached the public's attention faster than ever before. In today's world of instant information, a couple of keystrokes are all it takes to find all the information one will ever need on Wing Chun's history, on Ip Man, and the names of important figures who helped spread the martial art worldwide. For this reason, I do not wish to retell Wing Chun's history but instead, share some of its many treasures.

One of Wing Chun's / Wing Tsun's main attributes is its simplicity. It is designed to maximize one's movements through biomechanical efficiency delivering a fury of devastating attacks to an overwhelmed assailant in very close proximity. Short, fast, direct, and powerful. Following the infamous centerline theory, the shortest distance traveled is a straight line. Wing Tsun is composed of three empty hand forms, Siu Lim Tau, Chum Kiu, and Biu Tze. Throughout the student's progression, they are trained extensively in the sensitivity drills famously known as Chi Sau (Empty hand sensitivity drills) and Chi Gerk (Feet and leg sensitivity drills). The Chi Sau and Chi Gerk training allow the practitioner to redirect and subdue their opponent through body repositioning, limb trapping, and strikes at vital portions of the body.

The hours invested into the Chi Sau training allows the practitioner to develop a "Sixth Sense" one might say, to anticipate what their opponent's next reaction might be. Thus allowing the practitioner to be steps ahead of their opponent. Chi Sau and Chi Gerk are exclusive training exercises to the Wing Tsun System. Chi Sau can be compared to tennis, where proper timing, execution, and delivery have to be in sync with not just oneself, mentally and physically, but also with the opponent on the other side of the court, to overwhelm and nullify anything they may deliver.

Once the student is proficient in those empty hand forms, the following are then taught exclusively to high-ranking and dedicated students. The Mook Jong Set (Wooden Dummy), Luk Dim Boon Kwan (The 6 1/2 Long Pole Techniques), and finally the Baat Cham Dao set (The Double Knives).

One can learn all the outer shell of the forms and techniques of the Wing Tsun System fairly quickly, but to master it internally could take a lifetime. Practice does not make perfect but it definitely makes permanence. Without quality instruction in anything one seeks out to do, the sense of being in limbo is imminent. If one is willing to be a master in anything they wish to do, be it an athlete, a musician, an artist, etc, something worth doing, one has to devote their time and pour their all into their craft of choice.

I fell in love with martial arts ever since I was a child. I spent many hours doing summersaults, flying kicks, and playing with a variety of martial arts weapons. One day I saw Great Grandmaster Leung Ting (He is my Si-Pak or "師伯" in Chinese, the kung fu elder brother or "師兄" of my Sifu Cheng Chuen Fun) on television, performing Wing Tsun's Chi Sau (Sticky hand sensitivity technique) against a taller and more muscular individual, GGM Leung Ting neutralized every attack with ease.

From that very moment, I fell in love with Wing Tsun

Kung Fu. I thought to myself that this kung fu style is very well suited for me since I am relatively small in physique. Still to this day, I believe that this kung fu style and its theories and principles suit me and my environment perfectly. With Wing Tsun's compact movements, they are ideal for close-quarter places such as elevators, narrow hallways, stairs, etc., features that are found typically in the busy streets of Hong Kong where I grew up. Looking back, I have been teaching Wing Tsun Kung Fu for more than 35 years, how time flies!

Not only did I learn Wing Tsun techniques, applications, and theories, but I also gained a greater understanding of its principles, wisdom, and gained the ability to apply them in everyday life and my Wing Tsun practice. Mastery over one's emotions, having sound resolve in the face of adversity and the redirection of attacks are all techniques one can apply in life. I can still recall one of my kung fu elder brothers (kung fu elder brother or "師兄" in Chinese) sharing his experiences with me. It consisted of him applying techniques from Wing Tsun, specifically techniques of redirecting and deflecting incoming aggression. He overcame heightened emotions from a group of friends using Wing Tsun principles and theories. As a result, he was able to deescalate the situation. At the time, I was only a novice in my martial arts journey and have not yet fully understood the many nuances Wing Tsun had to offer. It was not until much later in my training that I realized how much my Si Hing understood Wing Tsun's principles, theories, and wisdom to be able to use them in everyday life.

It is my wish to share various examples of Wing Tsun's wisdom with those who may one day need them. In case one may find the need to adapt and overcome various life obstacles, struggles and challenges, it may assist them with the confidence and assurance needed for them to achieve the outcome they wish.

*** In this book you will see both the "Wing Tsun" and "Wing Chun" spellings used to describe the art. The "Wing Tsun" (WT) spelling is used by the descendants of GGM Leung Ting instead of "Wing Chun" due to some conceptual and technical differences from other streams of the late Grandmaster Ip Man's art. This book will apply the "Wing Chun" (WC) spelling when referencing the art in general.

Siu Lim Tau

Chum Kiu

Biu Tze

Wooden Dummy

Long Pole

Double Knives

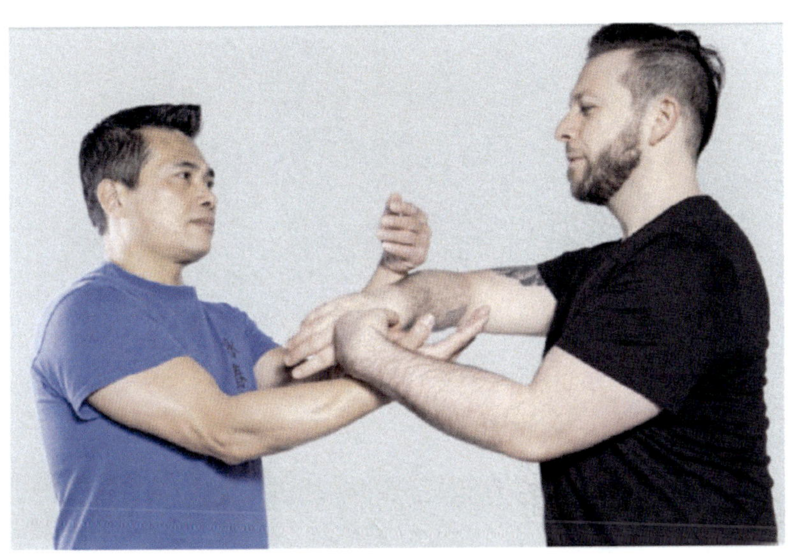

Chi Sau

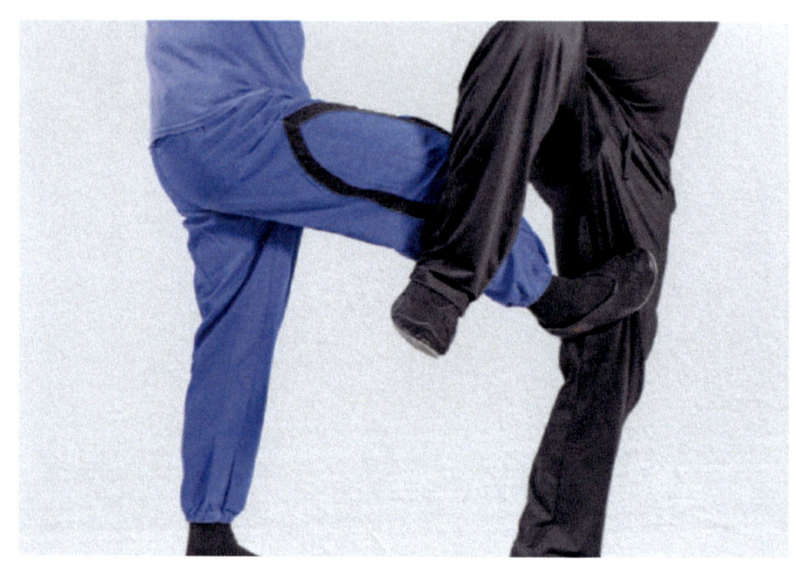

Chi Gerk

Acknowledgments

I am extremely fortunate to be a direct student of the two most renowned Wing Tsun Kung Fu masters :

Great Grandmaster Leung Ting and Grandmaster Cheung Chuen Fun

Throughout my Wing Tsun journey, they have poured unto me the entire system wholeheartedly, sharing their personal wisdom and philosophies on life. Throughout the years I have had the opportunity to meet many kung fu instructors including their students. All ranging from various lineages, many of whom I still consider dear friends. We have shared many conversations and laughs over the years. These relationships not only taught me the fine details about martial arts but also influenced me on how I teach my students Wing Tsun Kung Fu. Without them, my accomplishments, and my life today would not be possible. I am saddened that I have misplaced some of the photographs, and have lost touch with some of these friends, but the many fond memories will never be forgotten. My sincere apologies to those whose pictures I could not find at the time of writing this book. Thank you all for enriching my life.

Photo with Grandmaster Cheng Chuen Fun
and Great Grandmaster Leung Ting

Photo with Sifu Tam Hung Fun

Photo with Sifu Elmond Leung (U.S.A.)

Photo with Sifu Chan Pak Wing, Thomas

Photo with Sifu Leung Kwok Wah

Photo with Sifu Lee Yeung Chi, Albert

Photo with Sifu Wong Chiu Hung

Photo with Sifu Lam Yuk Doi

Photo with Sifu Li Yuan Tim, Timmy

Photo with Sifu Ho Fat Lin

Photo with Sifu Tam Yiu Ming (U.K.)

Photo with Sifu Lam Yuen Hang

Photo with Sifu Yeung Kai Kwong

Photo with Sifu Wan Kam Leung

Photo with Sifu Kwok Wai Yin, William (U.S.A.)

Photo with Sifu Chris Mah (U.S.A.)
and Sifu Steve Chan (U.S.A.)

Photo with Sifu Robert Torok (Hungary)

Photo with Sifu Wong Nga Chung

Photo with Sifu Phillip Chang (U.S.A.)

Photo with Sifu Alex Richter (U.S.A.)

Photo with Sifu David Brown (U.S.A.)

Photo with Sifu Dominique Emond (Canada)

Photo with Sifu Allan Sargan (U.S.A.)
and Sifu Ray Jurado (U.S.A)

Photo with Sifu Kong Chi Keung

Photo with Sifu Gilbert Leal (U.S.A.)

The Wisdom of Wing Tsun
詠春金句

Hands lead where you turn,
strike with elbows centered.

轉馬手先行
發拳肘在中

From a geometric standpoint, the shortest distance between two points is a straight line. Wing Tsun's theories and principles are based on the economy of motion using the shortest distance between two points. The fists and arms should always lead the change in direction while repositioning in a fight. Initiating with the arms serves as protection while repositioning. The arms also serve as a visual threat, a faint, a barrier preventing or even briefly stalling your opponent from getting closer to you, allowing you to adapt from a neutral position to a reactive one. Repositioning of the feet is also very important. Swift adaptability of your stance allows you to arrive at a position where your attack can deliver maximum force and efficiency. The fist and forearm should come from the heart, the center of your chest, in harmony with your intent. Doing so allows you to deliver your potential power, utilizing your structure, allowing you to defend strikes from different angles. One can neutralize an opponent's attack, and at the same time deliver an attack of one's own, executing true fluidity.

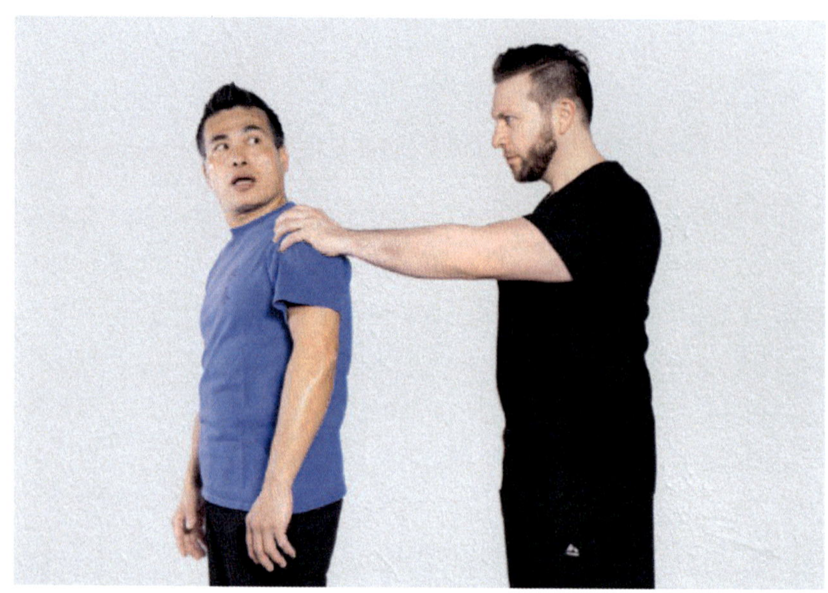

Photo (1): When you perceive the presence of an enemy behind you,

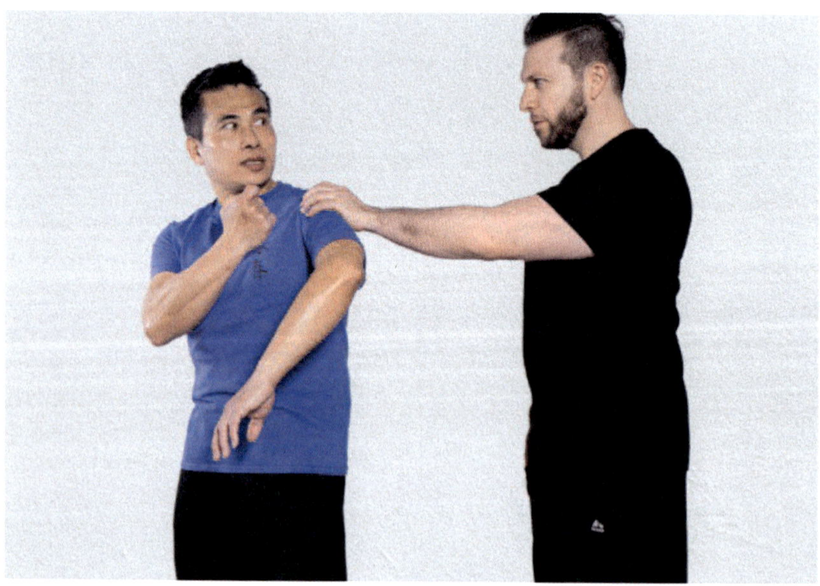

Photo (2): move your fist to the general direction before you completely align your body with the enemy.

Photo (3): The fist should be in the right position when aligning with the opponent,

Photo (4): it should make contact with the opponent by the time alignment is completed.

If the wrist rises the elbow descends,
if the elbow rises the wrist descends.

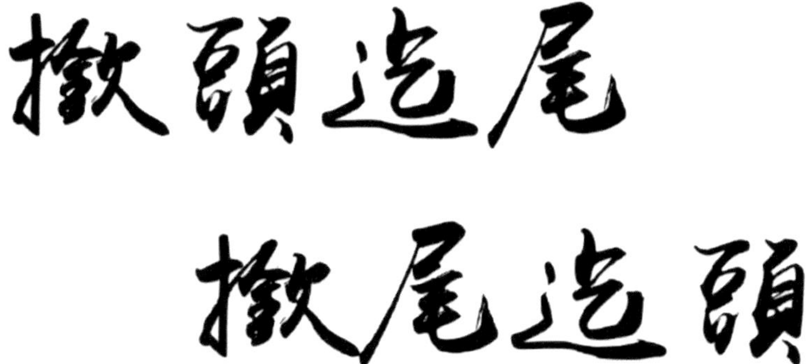

If one is on the receiving end of a fierce attack, there are only a couple of choices you have. One may confront it, give way to it, redirect it or surrender to it. The choice or reaction depends on the situation, the individual, and the environment. Preservation of life is the highest priority, do what you must to overcome life-threatening situations unscathed, for your loved ones and yourself. Wing Tsun Kung Fu is a martial art system that is simultaneously offensive and defensive in its approach when dealing with an aggressor.

There is one technique that stands out, covering the different scenarios of an incoming threatening force, it is what Wing Tsun calls the "Bong Sau" (膀手) technique. The technique confronts the attack, gives way for your own attack, while redirecting the incoming force.

The Bong Sau technique isn't executed, instead, it's a reaction. It is stimulated into a reactive state when there is incoming pressure to the wrist, causing the wrist to descend from its original position while simultaneously giving rise to the elbow. Coupled with a rotational motion of base and torso it also promotes redirection of the opponent's incoming attack. One may also imagine the forearm as if it is a seesaw, where one end rises as the opposite end descends. The opposite reaction to the Bong Sau technique is what Wing Tsun calls the "Tan Sau" (攤手) technique where the elbow descends while the wrist rises.

Photo (1): When the left wrist is controlled,

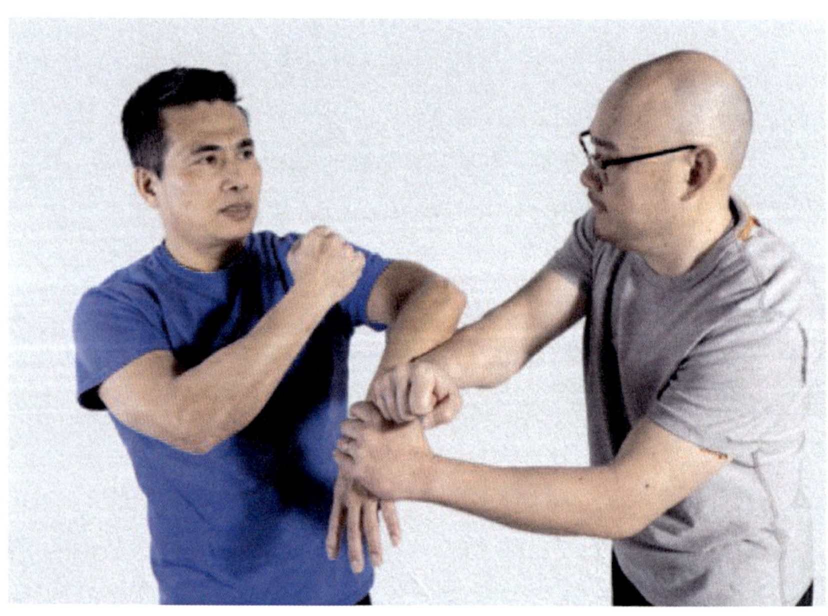

Photo (2): the left elbow rises into a “Bong Sau”.

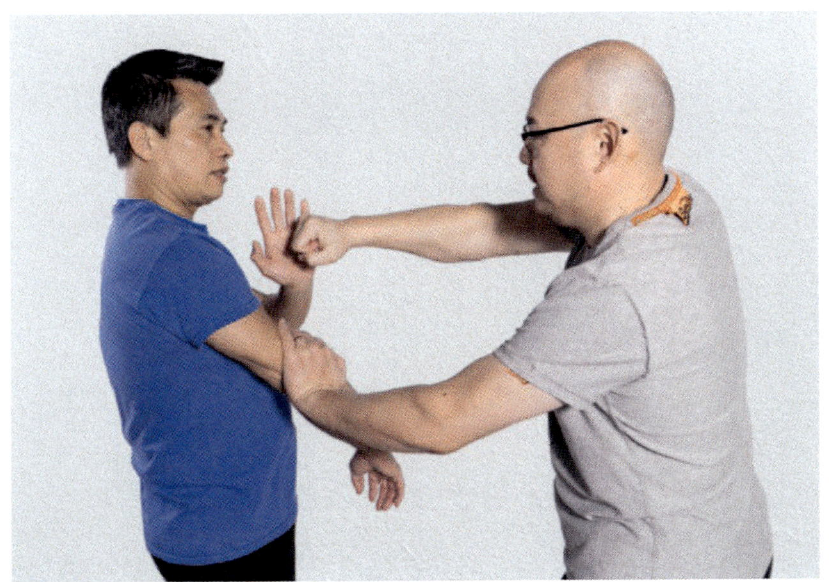

Photo (3): When the right elbow is controlled,

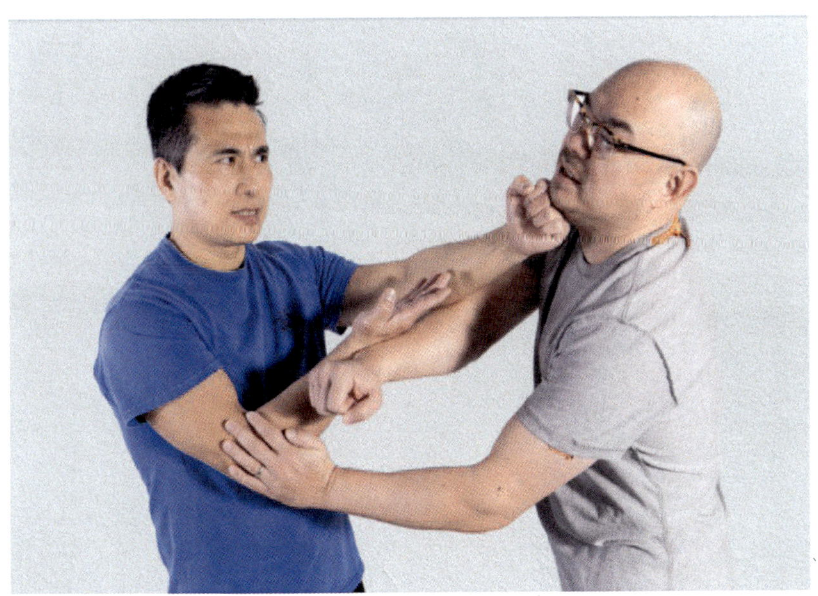

Photo (4): the right hand rises into a “Tan Sau”.

The body can be hardened,
the chin cannot, aim for the chin.

銅拳鐵臂鋼身軀
紙紮下巴玻璃頭

The Buddhist nun Ng Mui, was the founder of Wing Chun Kung Fu. She designed the martial art to be fast, simple, and lethal. Through proper diligent training and logic, one can overcome much stronger opponents, regardless of size and strength. Wing Chun / Wing Tsun emphasizes specifically on trapping and delivering overwhelming, close-quarter strikes to vital parts of an opponent's body. One of the most vulnerable parts of the human body is the head. Striking the face, in particular, can end the fight in an instant. Although there are vital targets on the torso and though it is a bigger target, sometimes they are not easy to get to and also not as vulnerable. With a well-placed strike to the head, one can end the fight instantly.

Photo (1): If you only attack the arms,

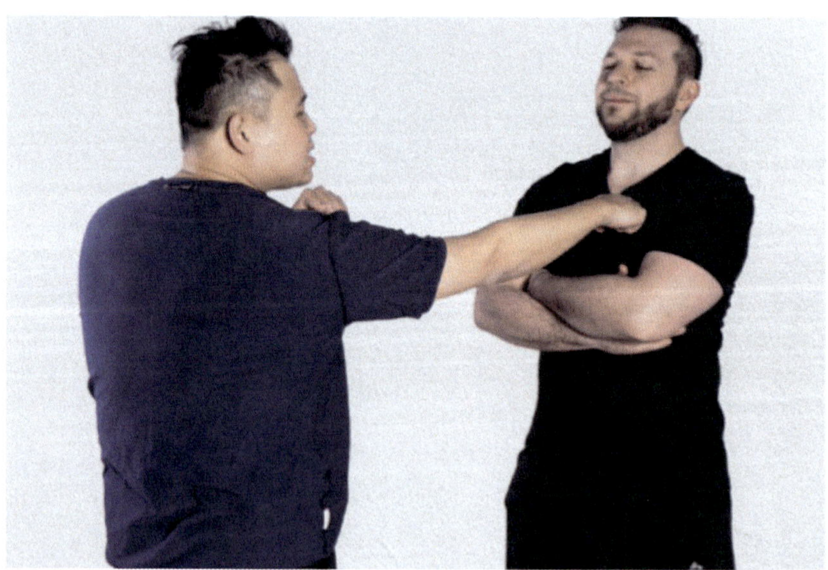

Photo (2): or the opponent's chest, they cannot be hurt.

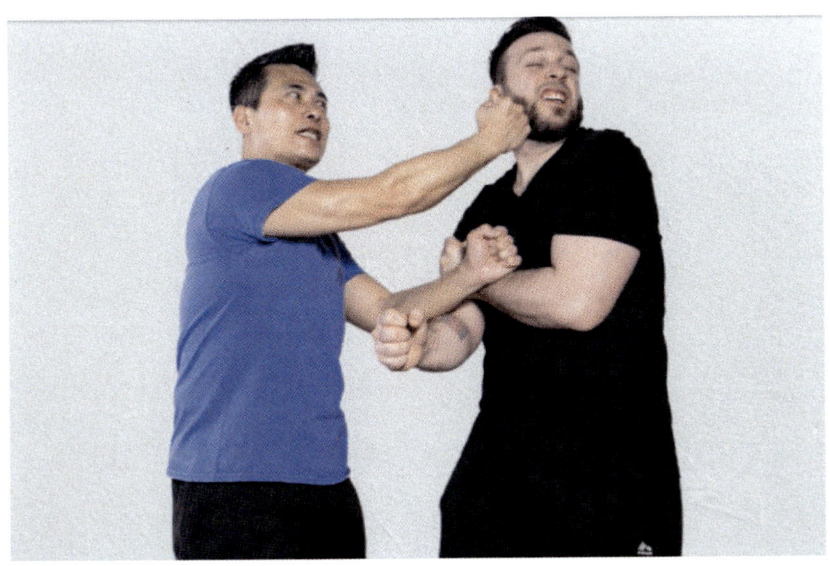

Photo (3): Concentrate attacks to weaker spots instead, for example the head,

Photo (4): or the jaw or the chin.

Traverse the string of the bow, not the bow itself.

人行弓背我行弦

One of the unique characteristics that set Wing Tsun apart from other martial arts is that almost all of the movements tend to travel the shortest path to their target.

The string and the bow analogy is one that deeply resonates with Wing Tsun's concepts. It reminds the practitioner to take the shortest path. The first two empty hand forms follow this concept, they both use very linear movements. The movements in the third form break that concept. A qualified, experienced instructor will be able to inform the practitioner why, when, and how to use those movements. Most kung fu styles tend to have very wide circular movements and require large spaces to execute them. The bigger the movements, the more time is given to the opponent to counter them. Wing Tsun compensates wide, extravagant, exhaustive techniques for quick, fluid, overwhelming ones. Power means nothing if the strike does not connect. It's not unusual to witness a Wing Tsun expert punching several times in under a second. In a fight, it's not how hard you can strike but how soon can you strike.

Photo (1): Pay close attention to the opponent's movements,

Photo (2): the opponent is about to attack with a left hook.

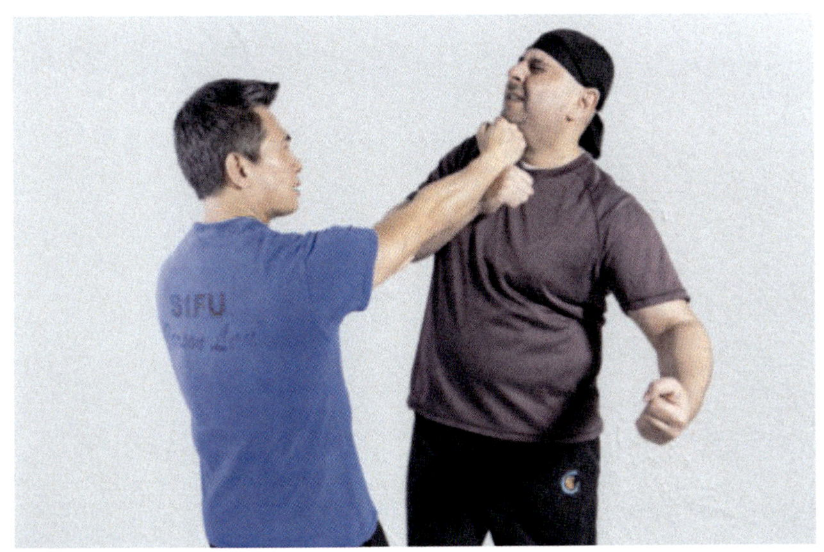

Photo (3): Then counter with a straight punch,

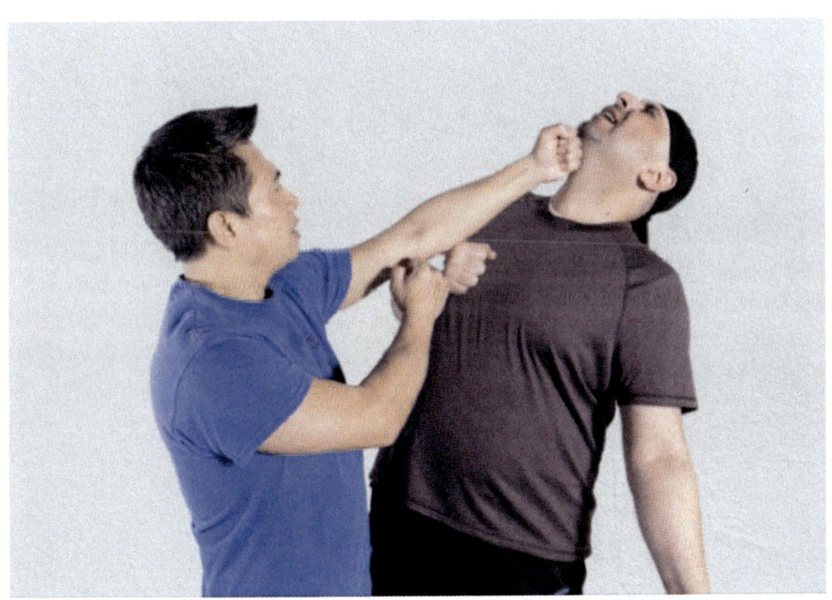

Photo (4): followed by forward steps and chain punches to exert forward pressure to knock out the opponent.

Power generates from the elbow, forearm and then fist.

發力在先力在臂
發力在後力在拳

Wing Tsun's punch is very unique. Unlike boxing and other styles of martial arts, the delivery of the fist does not twist before the point of impact. The fist stays vertical all the way through, commencing from the centerline to the point of impact. The three bottom knuckles, pinky, ring, and middle, are what mainly makes contact with the target. The elbow travels among the centerline throughout the entire delivery. The hand stays ready, not yet a fist and not yet relaxed, until the very last moment just before impact. The shoulders stay square on with the adversary, chasing their centerline the entire time. When punches can be executed quickly, one after another, that is what Wing Tsun calls "Chain Punches". Note that a clenched fist from beginning to end may reduce one's speed in unleashing the punch.

Photo (1): This fighter tenses up his forearm in an attempt to increase the power of his punch,

Photo (2): as a result, power gets trapped in the forearm when the punch makes contact with the target.

Photo (3): Instead, the fighter should relax his forearm and fist.

Photo (4): The forearm gets its explosive power from the elbow.

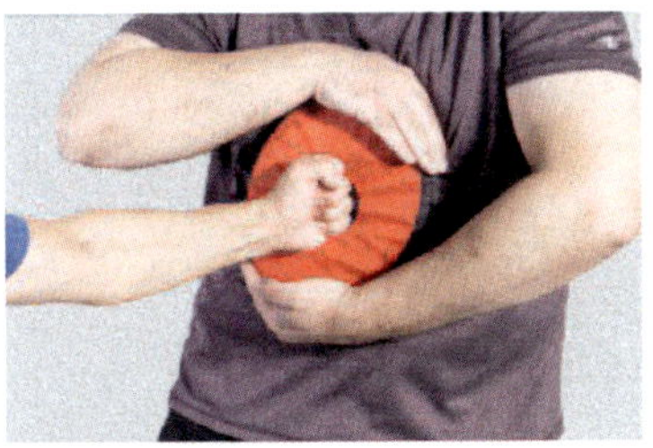

Photo (5): These types of punches can deliver lots of power over short distances.

Strike with confidence,
but not overconfidence.

As the good old adage goes, the best defense is a good offense. One of the best techniques used to prevent an opponent from attacking effectively is to keep them guessing and busy defending. In the game of chess, when one decided the move to make, then there is no going back to the same board as before. Pieces have moved. The competition for, and exchange in domination has begun. There is often an advantage to whoever initiates the first attack. One may, most likely, be able to determine where the fight goes and the overall final outcome. Beware of opportunistic gaps that the opponent can cease and control through possible counters. If the foundations taught in Wing Tsun Kung Fu are used, and the practitioner learns to move the body as one unit in perfect harmony, then it will become less likely for vulnerable gaps to be exposed. The system was designed to be fluid, chaining techniques together quickly and leaving opportunistic openings very difficult for the opponent to exploit against the practitioner.

Photo (1): The left fighter is afraid to fight,

Photo (2): so getting hit is unavoidable.

Photo (3): In a different situation, when the forearms are too high,

Photo (4): the opponent will be able to land a hit easily.

Photo (5): The proper structure is in using one's forearms to defend the torso,

Photo (6): remember that the best defense is a good offense.

Photo (7): Often a good strategy is to attack with "chain punches", and press forward at the right opportunities.

Striking fist on top,
retracting fist below,
punch to penetrate.

橋來橋上去
拳衝拳過軀

When closing the distance between two individuals, "bridging the gap" is the term commonly used in Wing Tsun. The forearms are usually used to close the gap. That's why the forearms are usually referred to as the "bridges". If one bridge is blocked, intercepted, or caught then the other bridge should instantly replace it from above. Think of them as the rods of the wheels of a train, where they constantly replace one another's space, constantly traveling forward. One gains the most advantageous position by occupying and controlling the space above the opponent's very own "bridge". If successful then one can seize the opportunity to gain free space for possible attacks. When attacking, do not just end at the surface of the target, but instead penetrate through it while always maintaining one's structure.

Photo (1): The forearms often come in contact during fights,

Photo (2): move the other arm above the contact point if one arm is controlled.

Photo (3): This makes it easier to attack the opponent.

Photo (4): One needs to take aim before punches,

Photo (5): and you must aim for a spot behind the target with the intention to pass through it.

Track the hands with your own hands,
strike when the way is clear.

有手黐手
無手追形

In combat, exchange and contact of the hands and forearms are inevitable. If an opponent is an experienced combatant, they may be able to manipulate one's limbs by gaining maximum advantage through positioning. If this is the case, one may not be able to easily control the opponent's limbs by simply chasing them. In Wing Tsun, we use Chi Sau "sticky hands" as a training tool to enhance and develop one's reflexes. In real-world scenarios, it can be extremely difficult to use Chi Sau to control an opponent's limbs. Do not obsess with what's in front of one self. Instead, maintain patience. The opponent will eventually reveal an opening. When this happens, seize the moment and travel straight through the centerline unto the target.

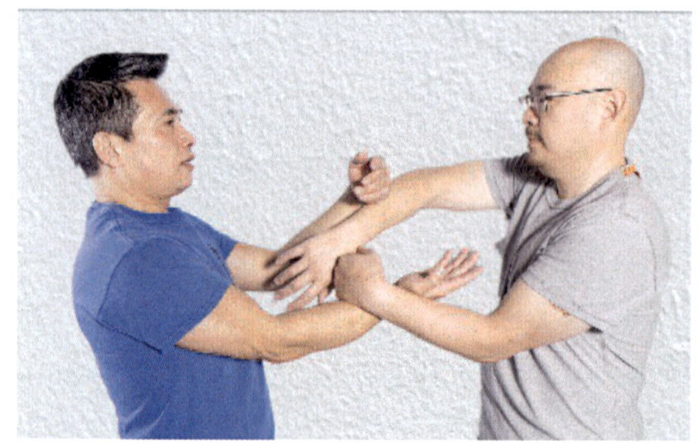

Photo (1): During Chi Sau encounters,

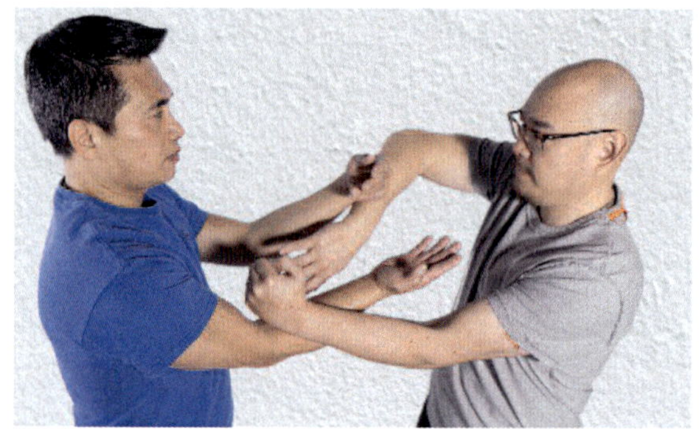

Photo (2): one can easily feel the opponent's attack while the forearm makes contact,

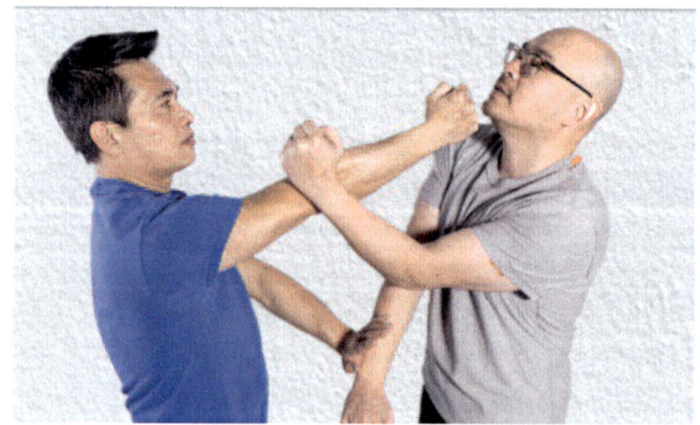

Photo (3): That way, he is able to attack the opponent and control his arms at the same time.

Photo (4): However, if the opponent moves away from your control,

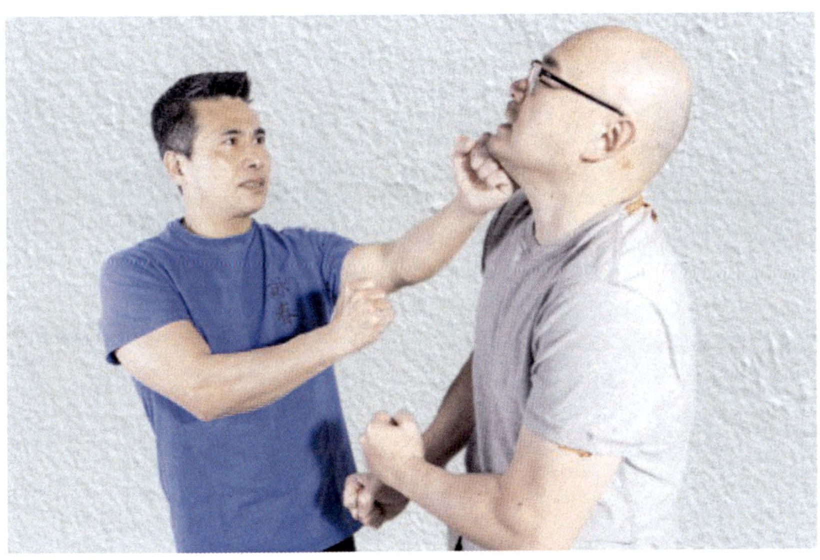

Photo (5): there is no need to attach to the opponent forearms anymore, instead, focus on attacking the center of the opponent's body.

The redirecting hand is a fluid motion, that changes defenses into offenses.

One of the most misunderstood and misused Wing Tsun techniques is called "Bong Sau" (膀手). A reactive technique that collapses into a semi-fixed position upon incoming pressure. To prevent your opponent from using your arm as a staging area, do not use your Bong Sau as a shield or a push against their incoming attack.

A common misconception when using the Bong Sau, is to use it as a stiff barrier between the aggressor and the practitioner. Proper rotation of the torso and stance must also be put into motion to redirect an attack away from oneself. Execute a counterattack, using "Fat Sau" (發手), a whipping technique, immediately after the Bong Sau. In a live fight, there is no need to meet an opponent's attack head-on. If done correctly, the chances of the opponent gaining control are greatly reduced if you redirect them to a different path instead.

Photo (1): During fights,

Photo (2): when the forearm feels the pressure,

Photo (3): use Bong Sau to divert the attack.

Photo (4): If the opponent continues to press forward,

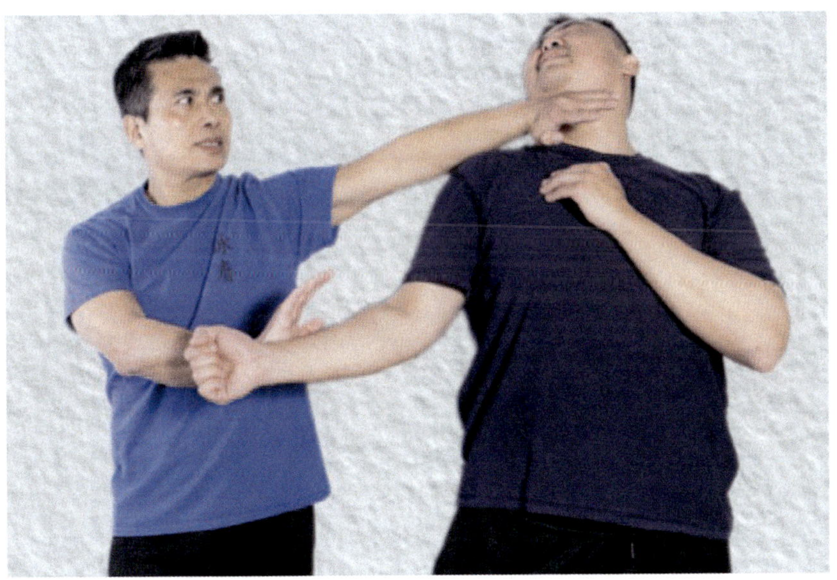

Photo (5): use the compression to counter with “Fat Sau” to attack the opponents neck or head.

Relaxation is the key to generate speed.

Many body mechanics need to happen to execute an attack. One can achieve speed and fluidity through a refined balance of body relaxation and muscle contraction. In a fight, a punch should not be seen by the opponent, it should be felt. If there is tension throughout the execution of an attack, the potential speed of a punch can be greatly reduced, giving the opponent a greater chance to see it and counter it.

A tense attack can be compared to driving a car while stepping on the gas and brake pedals at the same time, making it slow and predictable. It is especially important to have the forearms relaxed but at the same time ready to make a fist at a moment's notice. Unleash the power and speed that's created through proper body mechanics, concentrating all that force within one's fist and whipping it like an iron chain with an iron ball attached to the end of it.

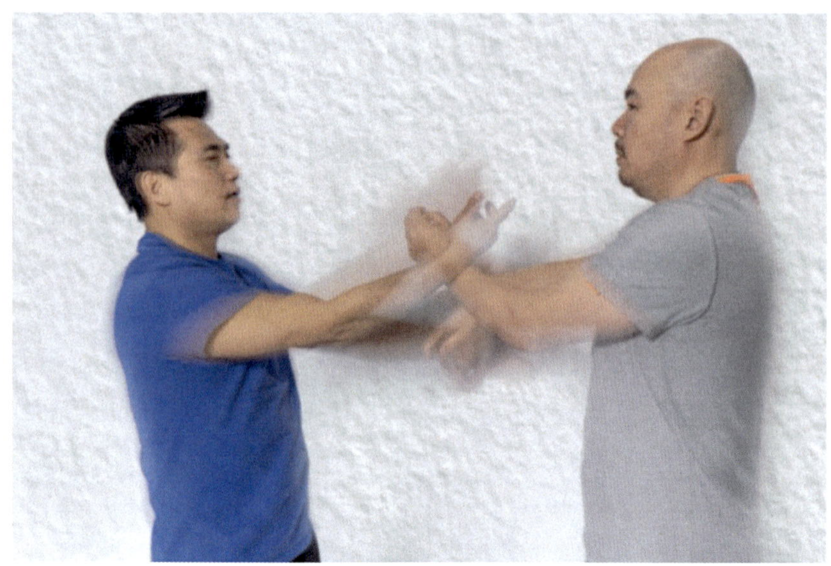

Photo (1): Attacks occur in an instant, moves are often executed at high speed,

Photo (2): the key to speed is relaxation.

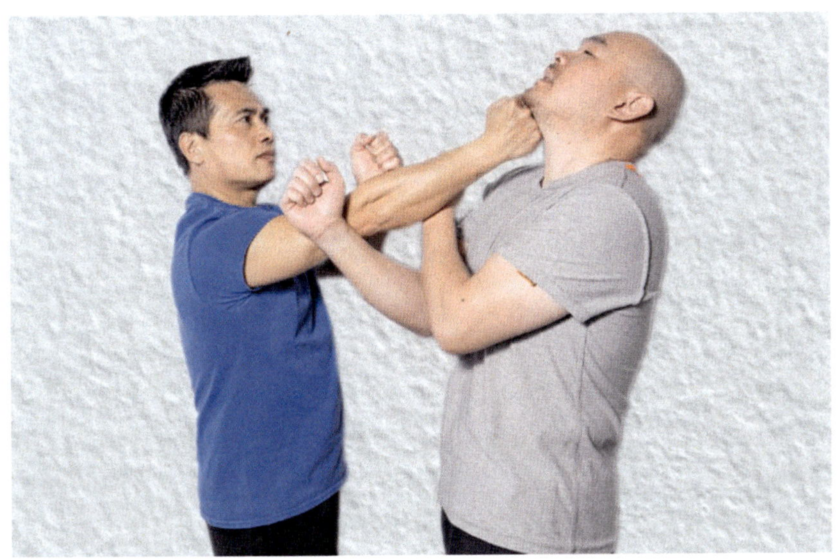

Photo (3): Most attacks should be aimed directly at the opponent's face.

Photo (4): An accurate and powerful punch can knock out the opponent immediately.

Photo Gallery

詠春教學點滴

相片分享

恒毅
梁木沉雄支廣廈

詠春

Performers : SIFU Carson Lau, Josh Midgnall, Ki Nosorthy, Daniel Cheung,
Dean Avallous, Giovanna Cioffi, Agnes Leung, Gloria Wong, Edwin Lau, Ben Li,
Chapman Fu, Matthew Chan, Simon Lo, Samson Wong, Alex Tran, Michael Lau,
Peter Tung, Anthony Kwong, Eugene Lai, Larry Lau

RONA

Walmart

ENCORE
Hill

Welcome
Master Carson Lau

BAY-MOUNTAIN
WING TSUN

TOYOTA
Road Service Debrecen

詠春

KICK & THAI-BOX-GYM
詠春

Final Thoughts

Many decades of my life have been dedicated to the word "kung fu". The books I have read and the movies I have watched... etc, all closely revolve around "kung fu".

Life obstacles are inevitable and unpredictable. Different chapters of one's life present diverse opportunities. Do not let opportunities to better oneself slip away. These opportunities may lead to success and may also lead to failures. Seize them. Learn from them. Conquer them.

Like Wing Tsun's Chi Sau training, one must also be able to constantly feel and maintain influence over not just one's surroundings but also one's outer and inner self. If found in a favorable position, always be ready to push forward with relentlessness, so new positions along with new possibilities may arise in your favor. If found in an unfavorable position, then do your best to redirect any external pressures. Stand your ground if ever faced with adversity, and resolve the issues at hand with a sound mind.

Of course, Wing Tsun doesn't just have the idioms related to empty hand forms mentioned in this book. There are many others, especially those related to the Long Pole Form and the Double Knives Form. So if this book proves to be popular, I might consider writing another.

I would like to leave you with a motto that I live by, one that has helped me overcome many obstacles in my life.

The one enemy you must always conquer is indolence, while the biggest challenge you will ever face is yourself.

Carson Lau

Credits

This book cannot be made by any one person alone, the brainstorming, layout, demonstration, editing and design ... are due to the inputs and dedication of our team. I wish to thank the support of all these individuals, names are not in any particular order:

Richard Ngai / Peter Tung
Gordon Shing / Zi Xin, John Li
Fernando Gonzalez / Raz Saremi

Last but not least, I would like to thank Raymond Law, Alex Richter, Chris Mah and Steve Chan for writing the forewords, their endorsements of this book is much appreciated.

Carson Wing Tsun Academy

160 East Beaver Creek Road, Unit #9
Richmond Hill, Ontario L4B 3L4
Canada

647-802-4982

www.wingtsun.ca

Made in the USA
Monee, IL
19 February 2023

28266253R00064